D1208746

HOLIDAY SINGING & DANCING GAMES

By ESTHER L. NELSON

Photographs by SHIRLEY ZEIBERG

Sterling Publishing Co., Inc. New York
Oak Tree Press Co., Ltd London & Sydney

OTHER BOOKS OF INTEREST

Best Singing Games for Children of All Ages
Dancing Games for Children of All Ages
Movement Games for Children of All Ages
Musical Games for Children of All Ages
The Rhythm Band Book
Singing and Dancing Games for the Very Young

To Fred Berk . . .
my lifelong friend and teacher . . .
with love

Thanks to Prof. Carol Reiman, Dr. Marian McMahon, S.C., and the children of the Children's Learning Center of Elizabeth Seton College in Yonkers, New York, and Director Mamie Williams and the children of the Williamsbridge Day Care Center, Bronx, New York. Special thanks to Lillian Enfield, Senior Educational Consultant for the Agency for Child Development, for being a constant source of encouragement, and final thanks to Sheila Barry, my excellent editor and great friend.

Cover design by Minn

Published by Sterling Publishing Co., Inc.
Two Park Avenue, New York, N.Y. 10016
Distributed in Australia by Oak Tree Press Co., Ltd.,
P.O. Box J34, Brickfield Hill, Sydney 2000, N.S.W.
Distributed in the United Kingdom by Ward Lock Ltd.
116 Baker Street, London W.1
Manufactured in the United States of America

Library of Congress Catalog Card No.: 80-52331
Sterling ISBN 0-8069-4630-X Trade Oak Tree 7061-2737-4
4631-8 Library

CONTENTS

BEFORE YOU BEGIN

When I was a young child, I really looked forward to singing that special turkey song as Thanksgiving came into view. Many of the holiday songs that we sang in school were not very understandable or meaningful to me, and yet there was the excitement of the approaching holiday and the fact that we made an attempt to celebrate it, even if the methods were not so great.

Actually, most of the holiday material that I was exposed to was old and tired and needed re-vamping. As I started to develop new material, I searched out some of the wonderful songs and dances that have been performed through the ages and passed down from one generation to another. I added dance to some of them, which gave them a new, lively dimension. As the Chinese proverb says:

> **"I hear and I forget.**
> **I see and I remember.**
> **I do and I understand."**

My favorite songs and dances of all kinds are in this book. Some are folk and traditional songs which we seem to have lost track of. Some of the dances are authentic and some are new. Some are games with music. And some are classics with a new twist. They all celebrate life and tradition; they take joy in ritual and repetition. You can play them anywhere—in the classroom or at home with friends and family. And everyone can take part, even starting with the very young. Take a look at the table of age ranges on page 72: several of the games can be played happily by two- and three-year-olds.

Come to them with the feeling of celebration. Pass on the joy to your young singers and dancers and players. They will carry it through their lives and want to pass it on to their children. It is an invaluable gift for life.

This New Year's bell is ringing to the right, all except Clarence, who has reversed direction too soon. Karla is clowning for the camera. She should be looking toward the center of the circle, along with the other children.

new year's day new year's day new year's

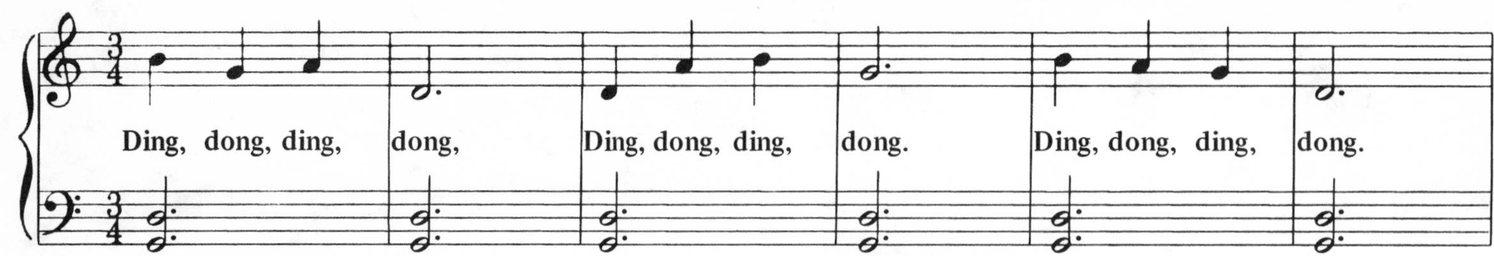

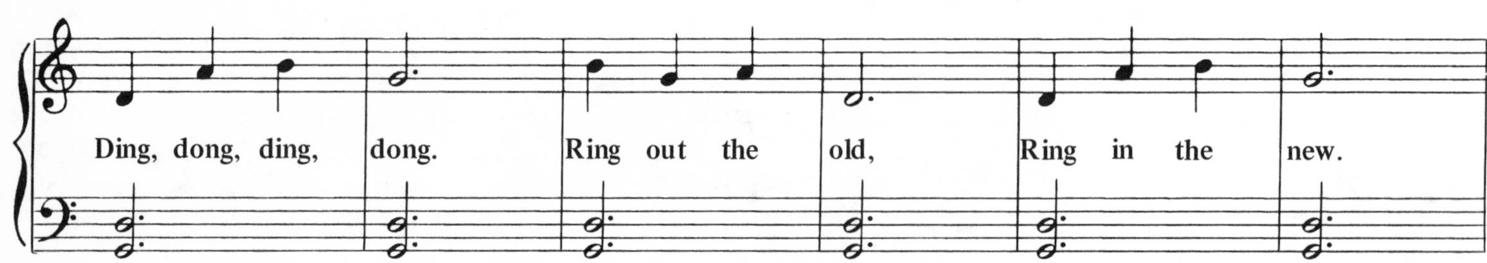

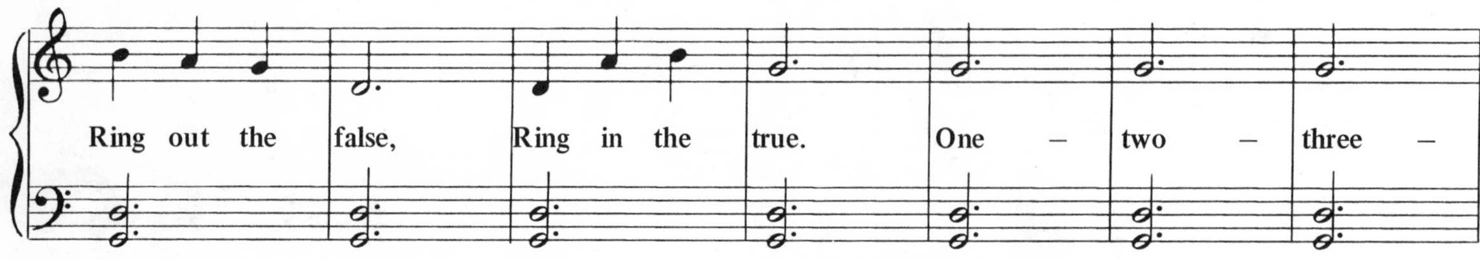

HAPPY NEW YEAR!

THE NEW YEAR BELLS

Number of players: 6-30

This English song is especially interesting because it has only four notes, repeated in different patterns. After you sing it, whenever you hear church bells, you'll listen for how many notes there are. (Chances are there will be only four.)

Ding, dong, ding, dong,
Ding, dong, ding, dong.
Ding, dong, ding, dong,
Ding, dong, ding, dong.

Ring out the old,
Ring in the new.
Ring out the false,
Ring in the true.

One—two—three—four—five—
six—seven—eight—nine—ten—
eleven—twelve—HAPPY NEW YEAR!

The feeling just before the New Year is one of closeness and friendship. So stand in a circle, arms around each other's shoulders, and sway from side to side as you sing. Each measure has three counts, so lean to one side at the start of each measure, and then to the other side at the start of the next. That gives you plenty of time to sense the group around you and the good feeling of moving together with it.

On the second stanza, instead of putting your arms around each other's shoulders, put your arms behind your neighbors' backs and hold hands with the next people in the circle. Keep the swaying movement going, but now that the circle is tighter, you get a different feeling from it.

After singing and swaying to the first two stanzas, and counting the chiming of the bells, from "One" to "Twelve," the New Year is here. Break your circle, shout "Happy New Year" and give everyone a hug!

OUT WITH WINTER (Push It Out!)

Number of players: 8-Unlimited

This game is based on an Indian game from the southernmost tip of South America. It is a land where winter reigns in December, as well as in June and July. The fog and damp and cold persist all year long, and the Indians keep fires going all the time. When the explorer Magellan saw the fires, he named the island "Tierra del Fuego," which means "Land of Fire."

You can play this game indoors or out. Divide the group in two. Put black eyebrow pencil or watercolor marks on the foreheads of one of the groups. These players represent winter. On the other group, put a green mark, which represents summer. To decorate the players further, if you like, draw circles or designs on their faces in the correct color.

Draw a chalk circle on the floor (or mark it on the ground, if you're outdoors), big enough to contain only one of the groups—the winter one. Now all the players fold their arms and keep them in this position for the entire game. The winter group is inside the circle; the summer group is outside. Now the summer group tries to push the winter group out, so that it can get inside the circle. Pushing with elbows is not allowed, only with shoulders and backs. No member of the winter group is allowed to step outside the line of the circle. If anyone does, he or she must join the summer group and try to shove the winter people out. The winter people can even sit in the circle, if they want, which makes it harder still to get them out. As the summer group tries to evict the winter group, this is the song they sing:

Out with winter,
We have had it!
Out with winter,
We don't need it!

We have iced
And we have frozen!
Enough of winter,
Let it go!

Be sure to draw the circle small enough so that the summer people can reach the winter ones. Each time three winter people are pushed out, re-draw the circle even smaller, so they become easier and easier to reach.

This game makes use of the players' ingenuity. Summer people have to be quick to see a chance to get the winter people out. They need to catch the winter people off balance, woo them, draw them closer and trick them. Be sure to warn the players ahead of time, though, about pushing only with shoulders and backs—and no tripping, kicking or hitting permitted!

OUT WITH WINTER (Push It Out)

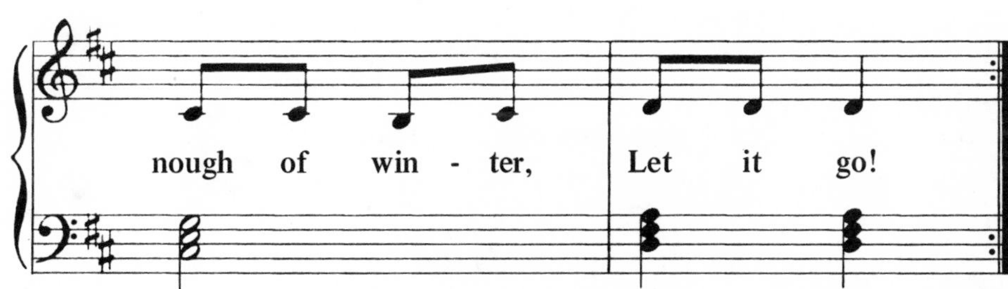

GYPSY IN DA MOONLIGHT

Number of players: 8-25

This lilting Caribbean singing game comes from Trinidad. The word "gypsy" is sometimes "tootsie" and sometimes it's the name of the child in the center of the ring, so you can sing "Judy in da moonlight," or "Georgie in da moonlight."

Play it with any number of people. It's easy and it can be performed by all ages, starting with the very young.

Stand in a circle. Don't hold hands: keep them free to clap as you sing. Choose one player to be the "gypsy."

Gypsy in da moonlight,
Gypsy in da dew,
Gypsy never come back
Before the clock struck two.

In the first stanza, Gypsy walks around the outside of the circle as the other players clap and sing and point to Gypsy.

Walk in, Gypsy, walk in,
Walk right in, I say.
Walk into my parlor
To hear my banjo play.

GYPSY IN DA MOONLIGHT

Gypsy walks into the circle in the second stanza.

"I don't love nobody
And nobody loves me.
All I love is Alice
To come and dance with me."

Gypsy sings the third stanza. On the line, "All I love is Alice," he or she chooses the name of one of the players who goes into the center of the circle.

Tra la la la la la,
Tra la la la la.

Tra la la la la la,
Tra la la la la.

In this stanza, Gypsy and Alice give each other both hands and skip around each other in a small circle. The outside circle sings "Tra la la," and claps. Then Alice becomes the new Gypsy. She goes outside the circle "in da moonlight," and the game continues.

If older children are playing, instead of doing a simple skip around each other, they can do any popular dance in the middle of the circle.

MASKED VALENTINES
(or Hearts of Many Emotions)

Number of players: 6-30

Valentine's Day is associated with feelings of affection, but there can be many kinds of valentines, and they can have many different feelings. This game gives the players a chance to explore such emotions and express them physically. It's not only a dramatic experience: it also develops creative ability, as each player moves in a unique way.

First, go through your records and tapes to find musical selections that have different emotional qualities: happy, sad, angry, silly, whatever.

Dancing Valentines should lean and twist in all directions. Patrice (left) is exploring the principle of balance. She is also moving her arms up and down and around. Bending and stretching your elbows makes for a whole new range of movement.

MASKED VALENTINES (continued)

You also need red hearts, which you can buy at a stationery store at this time of year. If you can't find them, cut them out of oaktag or some other cardboard. About twelve inches high is a good size for a heart, but you can also experiment with larger or smaller ones. They all will work, but you'll feel differently as you hold them.

Choose as many players as you have hearts, and give them each a heart. Ask them to hold it gently, between thumb and forefinger, at each side at the fattest part of the heart. The rest of the group sits in a corner of the room and watches.

When you start the music, the players can move their entire bodies—including fingers, wrists, elbows, shoulders, head, back, chest, hips, toes, ankles, knees, thighs—but *they may not let go of the heart*. They need to find ways of moving the heart, as well as their bodies, so that they're not in one place all the time. As they do this, they can move around the room on their toes, on their knees, on their stomachs on the floor, or jumping in the air, if they want.

Start the game by testing the possibilities. First you could begin with "Happy Hearts," and the players need to move that way. Play spirited music for about one minute. When the music stops, they must cover their faces with the hearts—like valentine masks—and hold that last movement facing the group. Of course, the rest of their bodies (the parts which are visible) need to look "happy."

The next valentine might be a sad one, but the same rules apply. Players now use their bodies in sad movements, and the music you choose should be sad. Their last movements, with their faces covered, also must be sad ones. Even though you can't see the expressions on their faces, you should be able to feel the sadness from their positions.

Now try "angry" valentines with big, strong, sharp movements, then "silly" ones with short, abrupt, funny movements. Ask the dancers if they can think of any other kinds of valentines to be. They will have lots more ideas.

Now the players hold their valentines high in the air, get on their toes, run once around the room, and finally give their hearts to someone sitting on the floor, who has not yet had a turn. The game begins again. Repeat it until everyone has had a turn.

If you have enough hearts for each player—and enough space—play the game all together. The second time you play, do it with partners, so that two players dance to each other, and end up facing each other, with their faces covered. Perhaps a third time, you can try it with three. That's a nice challenge!

OLD WOMAN'S COURTSHIP

Number of players: 6-Unlimited

In this delightful question-and-answer song, girls and boys form two separate lines and then face each other, so each has a partner directly opposite to sing to. The boys start:

Note: Each line is sung twice.

BOYS: **Old woman, old woman, are you good at spinning? (2)**
(*They do the movement of spinning by holding one hand in front of the chest and the other hand circling, first toward the chest and then away from it.*)

GIRLS: (*Cupping one ear and leaning toward their partners*)
Speak a little louder, sir. I'm very hard of hearing. (2)

Continue this pattern.

BOYS: **Old woman, old woman, can you do fine weaving? (2)**
(*They weave in and out with one hand.*)

GIRLS: **Speak a little louder, sir. I'm very hard of hearing. (2)**

OLD WOMAN'S COURTSHIP

BOYS: **Old woman, old woman, will you darn my stockings? (2)**
(One hand makes a fist—as if it was the stretched sock to be darned, and the other hand makes small sewing movements over it.)

GIRLS: **Speak a little louder, sir. I'm very hard of hearing. (2)**

BOYS: **Old woman, old woman, why don't we get married? (2)**

GIRLS: **Lord have mercy on my soul, I'm sure that now I hear you! (2)**

Another way to do this song is to have the two groups sing to each other, group to group instead of partner to partner.

Whichever way you choose, encourage the singers to enunciate each word very clearly, as though they're talking to someone who doesn't understand. Encourage them to over-react to each question—to mug, in fact. Before you even start the song, you can talk about all the expressions the face is capable of—using your eyes and eyebrows and mouth—and practice them, so the players are really free to let loose.

THE IRISH TROT

Number of players: 8-Unlimited

This dance is a terrific coordination builder. A spirited party game, it can use as many players as you have. Parents and children can do it as partners, too. Even if you have no music, the dance can still be successful, because voices alone can carry it. Of course, clapping will help, and stepping loudly in rhythm adds to the beat.

Form a circle of partners, girls on the right-hand side of their partners. The boys face the center of the circle. Girls turn half-way around so that they're facing away from the circle center. Everyone joins hands, moves a bit closer together and lifts hands high.

THE IRISH TROT (continued)

I

Hands all up in the Irish Trot,
Hands all up in the Irish Trot,
Hands all up in the Irish Trot,
Way down below!

The circle walks clockwise on this first verse.

II

Turn right back in the Irish Trot,
Turn right back in the Irish Trot,
Turn right back in the Irish Trot,
Way down below!

The circle reverses direction.

III

Rights and lefts in the Irish Trot,
Rights and lefts in the Irish Trot,
Rights and lefts in the Irish Trot,
Way down below!

Partners drop hands and face each other for a grand right and left. This means giving your right hand to your partner and passing your partner by continuing to walk in the same direction. Then you give your left hand to the next person you meet, and your right to the next, until you meet your own partner again. If the circle is large and you're still not back to your own partner at the end of it, sing the verse again.

THE IRISH TROT (continued)

Grand right and left

IV

We'll get married in the Irish Trot,
We'll get married in the Irish Trot,
We'll get married in the Irish Trot,
Way down below!

Note: for more about promenade position, see page 48.

Partners take regular ballroom dancing position, close to each other, and turn clockwise with each other in one spot. In order to do this, their inside legs (their right legs) must be close together.

V

Get a little pep in the Irish Trot,
Get a little pep in the Irish Trot,
Get a little pep in the Irish Trot,
Way down below!

Partners "do their own thing." It can be an Irish Jig or the latest disco step. Here there are no space limitations; they can use the entire room if they need it.

VI

Almost home in the Irish Trot,
Almost home in the Irish Trot,
Almost home in the Irish Trot,
Way down below!

Take your partner in promenade position and promenade once around the floor ("you know where, and I don't care").

ST. PATRICK'S POTATO RACE

Number of players: 6-30

This exciting elimination game adds to the festivity of St. Patrick's Day. If you're playing it with very young children (from three to five years old), line them up across one end of the room with space between them. Give each one a potato. Flattish potatoes are better than round ones, because the children must walk across the room with the potatoes on their heads—and very young children need all the help they can get.

Give a signal (a whistle, or clap your hands, or say "GO"), and the players start walking, trying to keep the potato from falling off their heads. It is an ambitious undertaking and chances are they will not make it, but it's fun trying. Allow them to put the potato back on their heads after it falls off and to continue walking across the floor. With children this age, it's best to take the race element out of it, and just let it be a game.

With six- to eight-year-olds: Play the same game, but this time, do it for real. If you drop your potato, you're out of the race. The one who walks all the way across the room with the potato in place is the winner. If two out of three racers make it, have a play-off with these contestants to see who is the ultimate winner.

If you have a large group of players: Arrange them in teams. Have the players walk across the room and back, and then give the potato to the next person on the team. As the players walk with their potatoes on their heads, trying to balance them, the other players sing this song:

Old MacTavish is dead, and his brother don't know it,
His brother is dead and MacTavish don't know it.
They're both of them dead, and they're in the same bed—
So neither one knows that the other is dead!

Just listening to these silly words adds to the difficulty of finding your own balance and walking a straight line with a potato on your head.

If the players are older—in the nine- to twelve-year-old group: You can make this game harder. Line up partners at one end of the room. Partners link inside arms. Place potatoes carefully on the heads of the first couple. As the music starts, they walk—arms still linked—toward the other end of the room. They have a time limit—the length of the song once through—to get there without dropping the potatoes. If either potato falls, the couple is out, and the next couple starts across the room. If they get across without any mishap, they give their potatoes to the next couple in line and go to the end of the line for another turn. The purpose is to eliminate all the couples. Last couple left wins.

ST. PATRICK'S POTATO RACE

THERE WAS A MAN AND HE WAS MAD

Number of players: 6-Unlimited

This silly song is especially appropriate for April Fools' Day. It's an adaptation of an old English nursery rhyme.

There was a man and he was mad,
And he *jumped* into a heating pad!

The heating pad it got so hot
That he *jumped* into a honey pot!

The honey pot it was so dark
That he *jumped* into a doggie bark!

The doggie's bark it was so loud
That he *jumped* into a big white cloud!

The big white cloud it was so high
That he *jumped* way up to the top of the sky!

GOODBYE!

Use this nonsense song as a jumping song. Take little jumps until the word "jumped" when you do a really big jump. Then make it harder, so that each time you "jump," you have to jump in a different direction. First experiment with it, using any space you need in the room, with no limitations. You can jump front, back, to one or the other side, diagonally or around and around.

SKIPPING MAD

If you find all that jumping too strenuous, skip instead until the word "jumped."

FROZEN MAD

For variety, choose one stanza during which the players stand absolutely still (frozen) until the word "jumped." This also gives you a chance to catch your breath.

AND OTHER MADS

There's Galloping Mad, where the players gallop until the word "jumped." There's Hopping Mad, where the players hop until the word "jumped." There's Turning Mad, Sliding Mad, and any other Mads your players can think of.

Older players can try this song in partners, working out interesting jumping patterns. If that goes well, try it in groups of four, or even six or eight. The group can do different kinds of jumps for each stanza. If the players remember them and are able to repeat them, they'll end up with a finished dance that can be performed later.

On the last line, don't forget to wave and say goodbye!

From the glowing expressions on their faces, you can see that these players love jumping! In their enthusiasm, they are waving goodbye with both hands. Chances are they'll want to do this fun song and dance again and again.

I'M A NUT

Number of players: 6-Unlimited

This nutty song for April Fool is especially good when you've been cooped up and need to shake loose.

I'm a little acorn, small and round,

A circle dance goes with it. Step to the right with your right foot. Then step behind it and put your full weight on that left foot. Continue this for seven steps. On the eighth step (the word "round"), stamp your left foot right near your right foot.

Lying on the cold, cold ground.

Now reverse the entire step. Start to the left with your left foot, put your weight on your right foot behind it, and move to the left for seven counts, stamping your right foot on the eighth count (the word "ground").

When you do the circle walk, bend the knee of the leg that steps to the side (your right foot when you go right, your left foot when you go left). When you put your other foot behind it, get up on your toes, so that you're moving down and up, like a fast horse on a carousel, as well as to the side.

People come and step on me.

On this line, start from the beginning, but this time do only two side-behind steps. On the word "step," jump (with both feet in place) and land with a loud noise.

That's why I'm so cracked, you see.

On this line, move to the left with the same side-behind step, but this time, speed it up double-time, so it becomes almost a gallop to the side. Stop galloping on the word "see," which means you have taken thirteen steps. This stanza is difficult, because it is not symmetrical as are the others. You really have to think ahead to each set of movements.

I'm a nut!

Drop hands and jump toward the center of the circle.

Tch, tch,

Stand where you are and shake your head and shoulders.

I'm a nut!

Jump back to place.

Tch, tch,

Repeat the head and shoulders shake again.

I'M A NUT

I'm a lit - tle a - corn, small and round, Ly - ing on the

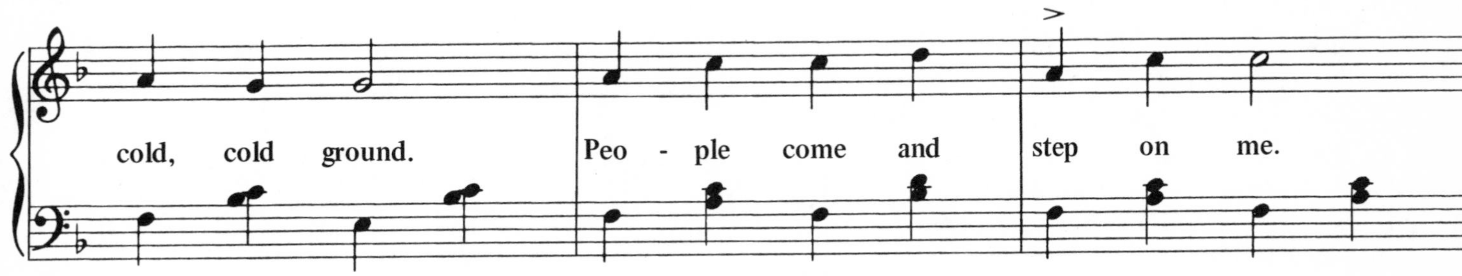
cold, cold ground. Peo - ple come and step on me.

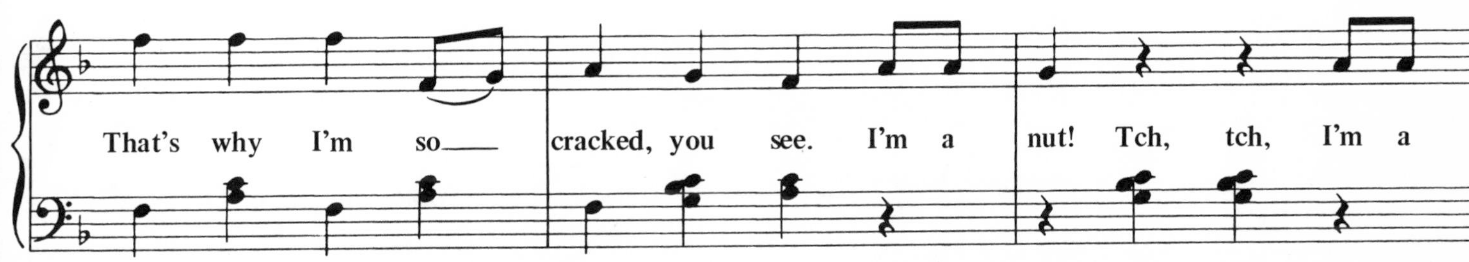
That's why I'm so___ cracked, you see. I'm a nut! Tch, tch, I'm a

nut! Tch, tch, I'm a nut! Tch, tch, I'm a nut! Tch, tch.

I'M A NUT (continued)

I'm a nut! Tch, tch,
I'm a nut! Tch, tch.

Repeat the jumps and shakes for these lines.

Then do the dance again from the start, for as long as you want to be a nut.

Give the players free rein to really get silly. They can sing in strange voices, mimic, act out, and generally let themselves go, but make sure the dance goes on.

There are other nuts besides acorns, so try varying the song by singing other stanzas instead of the first ones, such as:

I'm a little walnut, fresh and good,
I live in your neighborhood.

or

I'm a little peanut in my house
Sitting quiet as a mouse.

Try this easy version for two-, three- and four-year-olds: Join hands in a circle. Walk around to the left for the first stanza. On the second stanza, change direction and walk to the right. When you come to the word "step," all jump on both feet. Continue walking for the next half sentence, until the word "cracked," when you repeat that jump. Continue with the same dance as above for the "I'm a nut" part.

DAYENU

Number of players: 6-Unlimited

Passover is the Jewish festival of freedom, and it usually takes place in April at about the same time as Easter. It celebrates the passing over of the Israelites from slavery to freedom. The festivities begin with a gathering of family and friends at a special dinner called a "Seder" (pronounced *say*-da). This ancient Hebrew song is one of the most popular songs sung at the celebration. It is full of life and energy.

Ilu hotsi, hotsianu,
Hotsianu mi Mitsrayim,
Hotsianu mi Mitsrayim,
Dayenu.

Da-Dayenu, Da Dayenu—
Da Dayenu, dayenu, dayenu.

DAYENU

I - lu ho - tsi, ho - tsi - a - nu, ho - tsi - a - nu mi - Mits - ra - yim,
Ho - tsi - a - nu mi - Mits - ra - yim, Da - ye - nu.
Da - da - ye - nu da - da - ye - nu Da - da - ye - nu, da -
1st
ye - nu, da - ye - nu, da - ye - nu
2nd
ye - nu, da - ye - nu.

DAYENU (continued)

which means

If He had done nothing more than take us out of Egypt,
For that alone, we should have been grateful.

The refrain of "Dayenu" means, "For that alone we should have been grateful."

Use the first part of the song as a rhythm clapping game. Choose partners and line up so that you're standing in two long lines. Now drop hands, face your partner, take one step back and sit on the floor. You are now sitting opposite your partner. Designate one of the lines as Line #1. It will clap on the even beats. The other line is Line #2, which will clap on the uneven (syncopated) beats. Each group will clap eight times during the first two measures: Line #1 will clap only on the strong beats—One, Two, Three, Four and so on—while Line #2 claps on the beats *between* these main beats. These *between* beats are called the *and* beats, the *syncopated* beats.

The clapping should move quickly from one line to the other. It's like a fast echo, but both sounds are of equal volume. You really have to pay attention and make sure that you clap only and directly on your beat.

Practice this a few times. Play the music on the piano, while each line does its part separately, before you put them together.

Follow this pattern for the first two measures of the music (the first two lines of the song). On the third and fourth measure (the last two lines of the verse), both lines clap together, which makes it much easier. What they clap is

The rhythm is long-long-short-short-long, and they clap it twice.

The second part of the song—the Dayenu part—is a dance. Skip to it alone or with a partner, varying the skip so that it takes you forward, backwards, from side to side, on a diagonal, turning, or whatever and wherever you want. Clap your hands or move them freely. This freedom is a good release from the demands of the structured clapping part. At the end of the song, dance back to your places on the floor, face your partner and start the clapping part again. Look at your partner as you clap; the interchange is challenging and fun.

If you're working with an older group: Use a polka step instead of a skip for the dancing part. Try it this way:

DAYENU (continued)

1. Take three steps in place.
2. Hop on the foot that took the third step. Repeat this a few times until you know it well. Now you're ready for the real polka step.
3. Take a step to the right on your right foot.
4. Now step close to it with your left foot.
5. Step with your right foot in place and hop on it.
6. Now step to the left with your left foot.
7. Step close to it with your right foot.
8. Step again on your left foot in place and hop on it.

Once you master the step sequence, speed it up and really move around the room with it, turning as you go. It's an exhilarating step, full of bounce. If you do it fast and hop high, you almost get the feeling of flying. Just don't get so carried away with it that you forget to come back to where you started so you can begin again.

EASTER EGGS ARE ROLLING

Number of players: 6-Unlimited

This simple game is especially successful with younger children, because only one movement is involved and that is *rolling*. Now, rolling like a round egg is not so easy. You have to lie on your side, hug your knees to your chest and then make sure that you keep this position as you roll. Don't let your legs fly out and stretch, which is the natural (and easier) thing to do. You must really stay round and small and push your body over in order to make it roll. Once you master this coordination, you can do it without much thought.

Choose one player to be *It*. *It* stands in a corner of the room with eyes closed and fingers in his or her ears, so as not to hear the movement of the group. Then choose a Leader. The players will watch for the Leader's signal to continue rolling—or to stop.

Easter eggs are rolling,
Rolling down the hill.
Will they keep on rolling,
Or will they stand still?

For the first three lines, *It* stands still, eyes and ears closed, while the players roll around the room. On the last line, they look at the Leader and do what he or she signals—either keep on

These children are trying different movements that feel like rolling Easter eggs. Kimberly (left) is trying to be round by curling up backwards. It's important to experiment and find your own unique movements.

EASTER EGGS ARE ROLLING (continued)

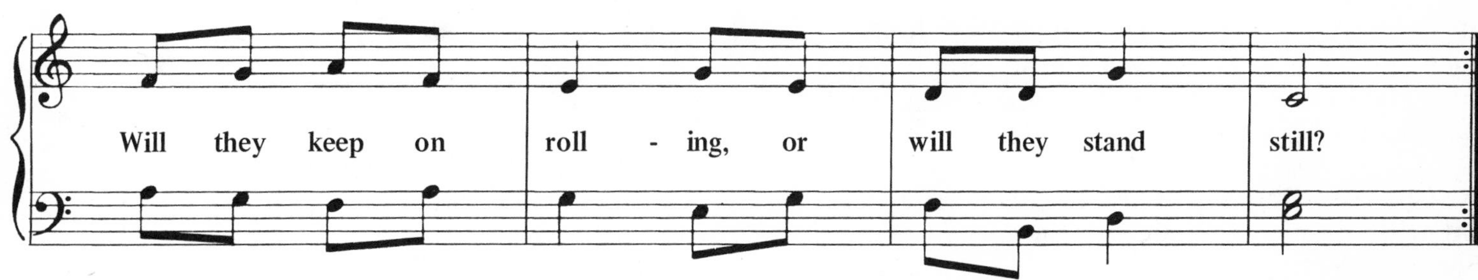

rolling or stop. At the end of the song, *It* has to guess what the children are doing. Then, right or wrong, choose another Leader, another *It*, and continue the game.

With older children (five and up): Try to find new ways of rolling. It doesn't have to be done on the floor. There are ways to get the feeling of rolling even while standing up. Partners—or even threesomes—can link arms around shoulders or waist to get into an egg shape. Just suggest a few of these possibilities before the players go off to create their own shapes and unique ways of moving through space.

TWELVE LITTLE RABBITS

Number of players: 12-Unlimited

This delightful song is great fun at Easter—or any other time of the year. The youngest children can take part: in it they'll learn to move on cue and follow directions. It's also splendid for learning subtraction.

Everyone is a rabbit and sits on the floor in one corner of the room, their old home. They will hop (when it is their turn) to their new home, which can be in any other corner, preferably one that is eight jumps away. Designate the corner so everyone knows where to go.

Before you start the song, choose the rabbits who will "hop away" during the first chorus. Then sing the first stanza.

I

Twelve little rabbits, sitting in their pen,
Two hopped away and then there were ten.

CHORUS

Hop, little rabbits,
Hop on both feet.
When you get home,
You'll have carrots to eat!

When you sing the chorus, those rabbits chosen will hop around the room and into their new corner. The hop should be really deep, so that the rabbits get way down with their bottoms almost to the floor. Stay down in the low hop; don't come up high again. Hold both hands at chest height, bent at the wrist and the elbow, while hopping. Eight hops are enough; then the rabbits rest in their new home. If this kind of hop is too strenuous, the rabbits can jump from a regular standing position, instead of a squatting one.

Now choose other rabbits to hop away on the next chorus.

II

Ten little rabbits, waiting at the gate,
Two hopped away and then there were eight.

CHORUS

III

Eight little rabbits, doing silly tricks,
Two hopped away and then there were six.

CHORUS

IV

Six little rabbits, shopping at the store,
Two hopped away and then there were four.

CHORUS

V

Four little rabbits, cooking carrot stew,
Two hopped away and then there were two.

CHORUS

VI

Two little rabbits found a new friend.
They hopped away and that is the end!

TWELVE LITTLE RABBITS

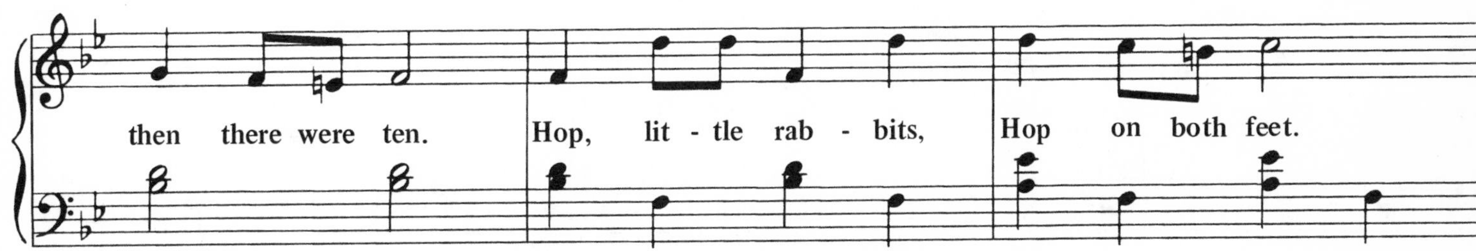

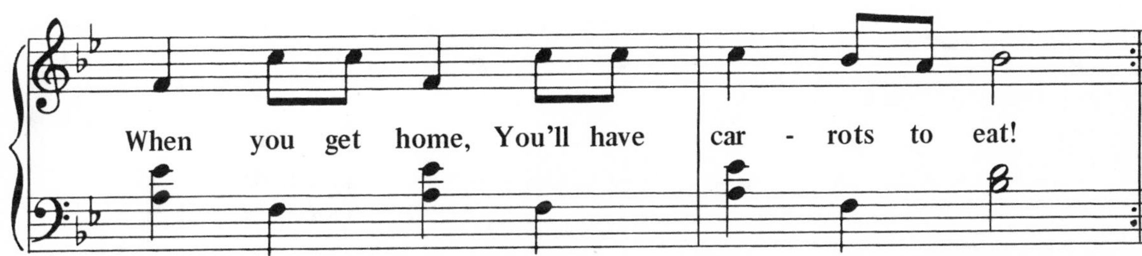

Chances are that you won't be working with exactly twelve players, so feel free to adjust the lyrics to your own needs. Three or four rabbits can hop at a time, especially at the beginning of the song, if the group is large. Then, as the song progresses, try to make it work out so that the number in the song corresponds to the exact number of players.

After the last stanza, when all the rabbits are sitting comfortably in their new home, repeat the chorus. Then all the rabbits hop around the room again, either back to their new home or back to the old one. Again, make sure you tell them which one to go to before they start out.

WIND UP THE MAY TREE

may day may day may day may day may day may

WIND UP THE MAY TREE

Number of players: 10-20

This ancient song probably dates back to the days when people worshipped trees. It was originally called "The Eller Tree," and the eller was considered sacred. There are many versions of the game that goes with it. The Indians in Virginia play it and call it "Rattlesnake." Another version is played on the streets of New York, and it's called "Wind Up the Apple Tree." The English version is "The Alley Alley Oh."

It's a challenging game to play. Six-year-olds may be able to handle it if they are mature. Seven-year-olds will have an easier time.

Start with the players standing in a loose semi-circle. The last person on the line is the May Tree, who plants his or her feet firmly and just stands still. The first person on line—the Leader—leads the line in a circle clockwise around the Tree as everyone sings, in steady marching tempo:

See the May Tree—what a pretty sight!
The blossoms are sprouting with all their might.
Wind up the May Tree and hold on tight.
Wind it all day and wind it all night!

The Leader keeps winding the line clockwise, circling the May Tree. As the circle winds, it gets smaller and tighter. When it is tight, the person next to the Tree stops moving. Each person after that stops moving and stands still, until they are all wound up tight, like a ball of yarn.

Note: As you wind up, stop moving before you're pulled.

When everyone is standing in a closely-knit, tight little circle, sing:

Stir up the dumplings, the pot boils over!

And everyone jumps up and down in place (you are all dumplings in the boiling water)! Sing this line twice, as you jump. Then the Leader starts unwinding by moving to the left with a sliding step. Everyone, still holding hands, follows until eventually the Leader has unwound the entire line. Be sure to pay close attention and follow the person in front of you, so the group doesn't end up in shambles on the floor (which, on occasion, is fun, too).

This May Tree has started its winding process. Nicole (the Tree—center) is standing still. Sean, the leader (wearing hat), has turned to make sure everyone is following him and holding tight. For this game to work, everyone must hold hands until the very end.

PLANTING RICE (Magtanim)

Number of players: 4-Unlimited

Nearly half the human race depends on rice for its existence, and planting rice is hard, back-breaking work. After the grain is planted, when the shoots are three inches high, the rice bed is flooded. As soon as the plants are six inches high, they are transplanted in a swampy field and kept in water until they are fifteen inches high. Then they are drained, weeded and hoed, and flooded again until the rice is harvested.

It's important to know how rice is grown if you're going to do this folk song from the Philippines. It dramatizes the whole process: the hours of bending, of having to stand in water and work all day in muddy fields. The people would sing this song as they worked to help them to keep up a regular rhythm. Sometimes rice field owners even hired musicians to play and sing as the workers planted.

This song in Tagalog (the Philippine language) is also well known in Hawaii.

I

Planting rice is never fun,
Bent from morn till set of sun.
Cannot stand and cannot sit,
Cannot rest for a little bit.

Line up to work, moving slowly, like the rice planters in a long row. Bend, take the shoot, dig a hole for it, plant it, and pat down the wet mud around it. Do this first to one side, then to the other. Then step back and plant another shoot and another.

CHORUS

Planting rice is no fun,
Bent from morn till set of sun.
Cannot sit, cannot stand,
Plant the seedlings all by hand.

Take a make-believe hoe and hoe the rice. Pull the hoe toward you with each movement. Hoe the rice on one side of you, then the other. Then step back and repeat the movements.

II

Oh, my back is like to break!
Oh, my bones with dampness ache.
And my legs are numb and set,
From all the soaking in the wet.

Stretch your muscles and massage all the sore parts of your body. Reach your arms up high. Then massage one leg with both hands, bending your knee and lifting it a bit off the ground. Then rub the other leg. Also rub your arms, which are tired from all the planting.

CHORUS

Do the hoeing movements again.

PLANTING RICE (continued)

If you want to sing this song in Tagalog, it goes like this:

Magtanim di ay di bi-ro,
Mag-ha-pon kang na-ka-yu-ko,
Di na-man ma-ka-u-po,
Di na-man ma-ka-ta-yo.

CHORUS
Magtanim di bi-ro,
Mag-ha-pon na-ka-yu-ko,
Di na-man ma-ka-u-po,
Di na-man ma-ka-ta-yo.

JA POSEJAH LUBENICE (I Planted Watermelons)

Number of players: 8-Unlimited

Here the work is the planting of watermelons. This delightful song is sung to a kolo, one of the most famous dances of Yugoslavia. This kolo is especially popular with Serbian children.

Ja posejah lubenice,
Pokraj rode studenice,
Seno, slama, seno, slama,
Zob, zob, zob, zob, zob, zob.

Jecam zito sedam i po,
A kukuruz devet i po,
Seno, slama, seno, slama,
Zob, zob, zob, zob, zob, zob.

which means

Watermelons will be growing
By the cool river.
Hay and straw, hay and straw,
Oats, oats, oats, oats, oats, oats.

Seven acres of wheat and barley,
Nine acres of corn,
Hay and straw, Hay and straw,
Oats, oats, oats, oats, oats, oats.

THE BASIC KOLO STEP

Each step has two parts: a step and then a bend on that same foot, in place.

Try the step first, to the right. Step on your right foot and then bend it. As you bend it, your left leg will come off the floor and bend behind you. Then step on your left foot and repeat. Be sure to bend only your knees; the rest of your body should remain strong, straight, and very proud.

PLANTING RICE (continued)

JA POSEJAH LUBENICE (continued)

Hold hands and form a small tight circle. Since the circle is small and you are close to the people on either side of you, you'll be able to feel the entire circle move as you do, as if in one piece. The circle steps together and bends together, and there is a feeling of strength in those synchronized movements.

Ja posejah lubenice,

Do four kolo steps to the right. End up with your weight on your left foot.

Pokraj rode studenice,

Change direction and take four kolo steps to the left. Changing direction calls for crossing your right foot and your whole body way over to the other side. It's like a strong twist of your entire body as you turn. It's fun to do it alone, but it's exciting to feel the momentum when the group does it in unison.

Note: If very young children are doing the kolo step, they can take four steps in each direction, starting on either foot.

Seno, slama, seno, slama,

Facing the center of the circle, on the word "seno," step right (to the side). On the word "slama," step left. Repeat this.

Zob, zob, zob, zob, zob, zob.

Stand in place and clap three times. Repeat this, take hands, and you're ready to start again.

THERE WAS AN OLD WITCH

Number of players: 5-Unlimited

This traditional English song is dramatic and exciting when you simply sing it. Move to it and it's even better. Everyone loves being a wicked old witch—nasty and hateful—with full permission. Do the song all together, so that each person can act out all the parts.

Start off with the witch, who does all the things in the first two stanzas:

There was an old witch,
Believe it, if you can,
She tapped on the window,
And she ran, ran, ran.

She ran helter skelter
With her toes in the air,
Cornstalks flying
From the old witch's hair.

Before you start moving, get everyone to talk about what a witch is like. Your first impulse is to screw up your face and look mean, but you need to go further and explore how a witch moves—in short, sharp, staccato movements. Experiment by doing sharp movements with each part of your body: your fingers, head, wrists, elbows, shoulders, chest, hips, knees, ankles, toes. Then put them together in sharp total-body movements. Act out the lines of the first two stanzas, with the players doing their own versions. There are no "right" movements; they are *all* right.

"Swish," goes the broomstick.
"Meow," goes the cat.
"Plop," goes the hop-toad,
Sitting on her hat.

Now the players all become other Halloween characters—the broomstick, the cat and the toad—as they appear in the song. Again, talk about and explore the movements of these creatures so that you really get the feel of them and can move into them quickly when each one speaks.

"Whee," chuckled I,
"What fun, fun, fun,
Halloween night
When the witches run!"

On this stanza, the players become themselves and do just what they please.

A second way to do this song is to give out specific parts. Choose one player to be the witch and then, depending on the size of the group, choose others to be broomsticks, cats, and hop-toads. Players move only when the song refers to them. On the last stanza, all can join in and move together.

THERE WAS AN OLD WITCH

There was an old witch, Be - lieve it if you can, She

tapped on the win - dow, And she ran, ran, ran. She

ran hel - ter skel - ter with her toes in the air, Corn - stalks fly - ing from the

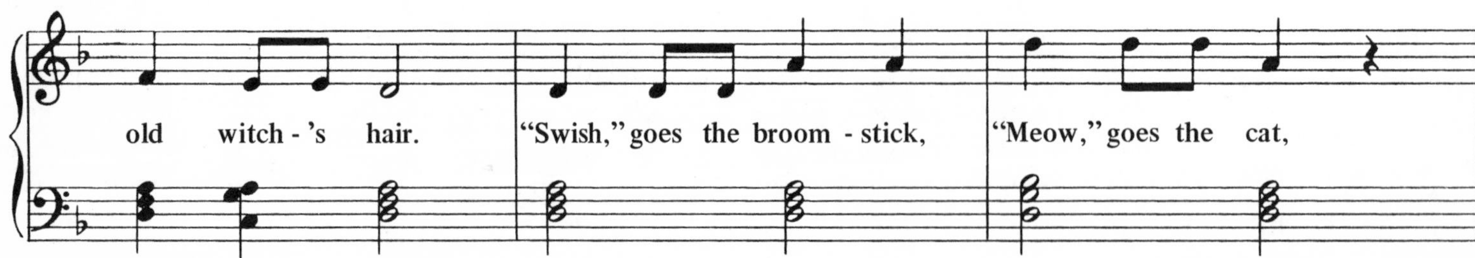
old witch - 's hair. "Swish," goes the broom - stick, "Meow," goes the cat,

THERE WAS AN OLD WITCH

Another idea: Instead of singing the song, the group can chant it, like a chorus. There is plenty of room for emotion and drama in the words. Don't be afraid to use weird rhythms and a wide range of expression to make it sound interesting and unusual. You can add words, too. For example, when you say, "Swish," goes the broomstick, you can add "Swish, swish, swish," after the word "broomstick." Continue this way with the entire stanza, adding the first word three times after each line. Play with the possibilities. Before you're through, chances are you'll have a fascinating presentation for a Halloween program.

Igor (left) is moving like a sharp, mean witch, with his crooked elbow and tilted head. Robert (right) is also using his hips as part of the dynamic diagonal movements. Jason (center) is moving his body in a crooked way, but he looks too happy to be the wicked witch. Next time he'll make his face sharp, too.

GHOST SONG

Number of players: 8-Unlimited

This eerie song is great fun and splendid for developing a dramatic quality in your voice, but it may be too scary for children under six.

Divide the group into two parts. One will do the singing while the other adds the scary refrain after each line. The refrain:

Whoo . . . Whoo . . . Yaaaaaah!

should be done in a high shrieking voice, but encourage the children to experiment when they sing it (or speak it) in a voice that ranges from high to low. The players who sing the words should do it in a quiet, hesitant voice, so that the contrast with the wild refrain is a sharp one. Be sure to reverse parts the next time you sing it: everyone wants a chance at the refrain.

The woman stood at the old church door.
WHOO . . . WHOO . . . YAAAAAAH!

And she had not been there before.
WHOO . . . WHOO . . . YAAAAAAH!

Oh, six long corpses were carried in.
WHOO . . . WHOO . . . YAAAAAAH!

So very long and very thin
WHOO . . . WHOO . . . YAAAAAAH!

The woman to the corpses said,
WHOO . . . WHOO . . . YAAAAAAH!

"Will I be thus when I am dead?"

Here, instead of the usual refrain, SCREAM!

I DON'T WANT NO MORE OF ARMY LIFE (Grand March)

Number of players: 8-Unlimited

Veterans Day or Armistice Day celebrates the end of World War I. This popular army song lets off steam and is loads of fun to sing. It is also an excellent marching song, with a strong, firm rhythm that carries you along with it.

Start by marching single file, Indian-style, around the room in different formations. Then take that single line marching down the center of the room, and when you get to the wall, "cast off." This means that the first person goes to the right, the second to the left, third to the right, and so on. It might be helpful to have someone stand at the head of the line to direct traffic, helping the players to go in the right direction. Each person, off to the side, walks around the outside and back to the center (at the other end of the room) where he or she matches up with the other line. Now you march down the center as couples, and this time, each *couple* casts off. Now when you meet at the back, you hook onto another couple, so that you go marching down the center in four's. You can continue this for as long as you have people, and finally send in one long line marching down the center. Then just march in place. You won't have to ask everyone to sing "loud and clear" here. It comes naturally.

They say that in the army
The drinks are mighty fine.
You ask for Coca-Cola,
They give you turpentine.

CHORUS

Oh, I don't want no more of army life.
Gee, Mom, I want to go—
Hey, Mom, I want to go—
Gee, Mom, I want to go home!

The coffee that they give us,
They say is mighty fine,
It's good for cuts and bruises
And tastes like iodine.

CHORUS

They say that in the army
The rolls are mighty fine,
One fell off the table
And killed a friend of mine.

CHORUS

The clothing that they give us,
They say is mighty fine,
Me and my buddy
Can both fit into mine.

CHORUS

They say that in the army
The pay is mighty fine.
They give you fifty dollars
And take back forty nine.

If the group is large and the Grand March is still going on when the words of the song run out, just hum the stanzas and sing the chorus.

I DON'T WANT NO MORE OF ARMY LIFE

veterans day veterans day veterans day veterans day

CAPTAIN JINKS OF THE HORSE MARINES

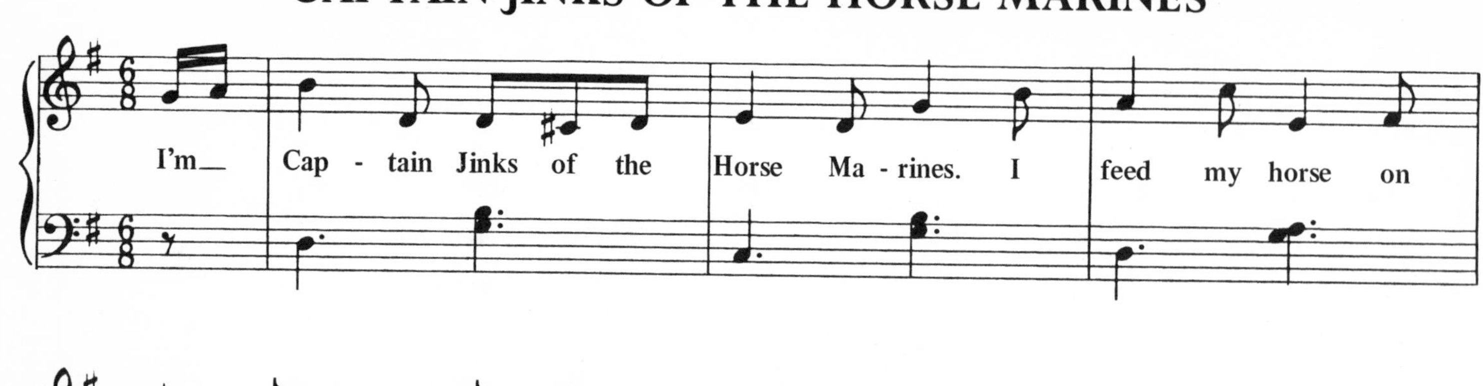

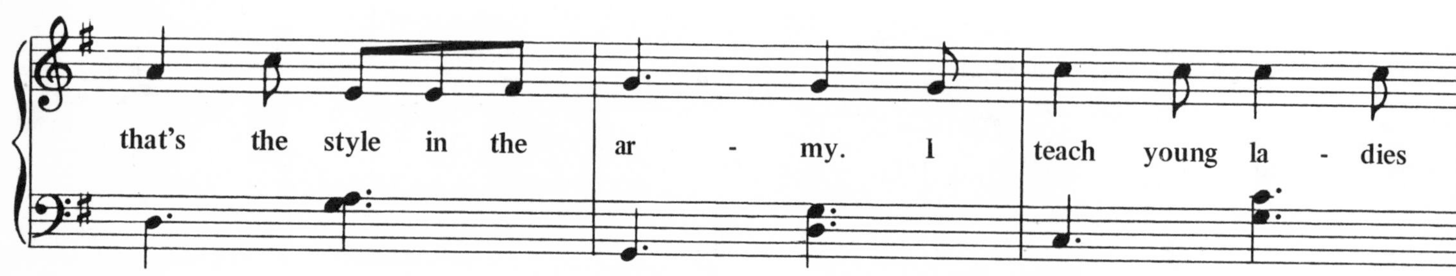

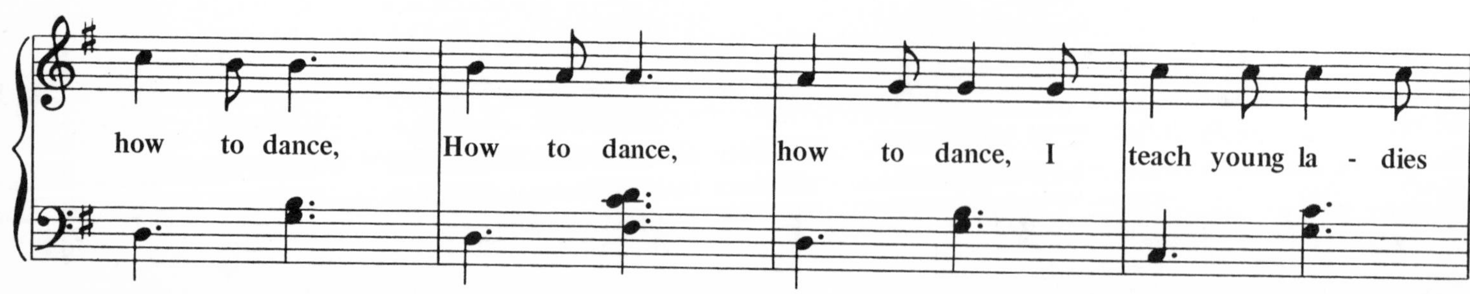

CAPTAIN JINKS OF THE HORSE MARINES

Number of players: 8-Unlimited

Many songs have been written about soldiers, and Captain Jinks is a special favorite. He takes care of his horse, as well as the young girls, and he sounds like quite a man about town. But apparently his mother thought otherwise, because another stanza says:

When he left home, mama she cried,
Mama she cried, mama she cried.
When he left home, mama she cried,
"He's not cut out for the army!"

Do this dance in couples in a single circle. Everyone faces the circle center, stamps one foot and claps hands and sings these two verses:

"I'm Captain Jinks of the Horse Marines.
I feed my horse on corn and beans,
And court young ladies in their teens,
For that's the style in the army.

I teach young ladies how to dance,
How to dance, how to dance,
I teach young ladies how to dance,
For that's the style in the army!"

That clapping and stamping is done to the original version of "Captain Jinks."

Here is the square dance version.

I

When Captain Jinks comes home at night,
He claps his hands with all his might.
Salute your partner, smile so bright,
For that's the style in the army.

On the first two lines, clap your hands. On the last two, bow to (salute) your partner and smile "real loud."

CAPTAIN JINKS OF THE HORSE MARINES (continued)

II

Join your hands and forward all,
Backward all, backward all.
Join your hands and forward all,
For that's the style in the army.

Everyone holds hands and walks four steps into the center of the circle and four steps out. Repeat this on the last two lines.

III

When Captain Jinks comes home at night,
The gentleman passes to the right.
Swing your partner so polite,
For that's the style in the army.

On the first line, partners face each other and bow. On the second line the gentleman crosses in front of his own partner and takes the next lady on the right as his new partner. He swings that lady (a real square dance swing). If you're working with children under seven, a two-handed skip around is fine.

IV

Promenade all around the hall,
Around the hall, around the hall.
Promenade all around the hall,
For that's the style in the army!

To take a promenade position: Face to the right. Partners take each other's right hands, and then

Promenade position

left hands, so they are in a skating position with arms crossed in front. They now walk or skip or polka, going counter-clockwise around the circle. Depending on how large the circle is, they will probably arrive back where they started by the end of the music.

The dance is now ready to start again. If the partners arrive before the music is over, they can just bow to each other. Since Captain Jinks was a ladies' man, and very fickle with the girls, it makes good sense to repeat this dance with new partners until everyone is tired.

When you've done the dance as many times as you want, stand in place, stamp one foot and clap your hands as you sing the song once through from "I'm Captain Jinks" to the last "style in the army." Then go back to "I'm Captain Jinks" and sing it halfway through to the *first* "style in the army." Slow down the last line so that everyone can feel the song coming to an end.

CREEK RIBBON DANCE

Number of players: 8-Unlimited

Feasts of Thanksgiving are celebrated all over the world. This sacred dance is part of a ritual of thanksgiving for plentiful crops. It comes from an Indian tribe in the southern part of the United States (mainly Alabama and Georgia), the Creek Indians, who are thought to be descended from the Mayans of South America. They were farmers who raised corn, beans, squash and tobacco.

CREEK RIBBON DANCE (continued)

This Creek Ribbon Dance is done by women on the first day of the annual Green Corn ceremonies. Ribbons of many colors are attached to their headpieces and dresses, which makes for a colorful dance. Turtle shells filled with small rocks are attached around their ankles, which make a rattling sound when the dancers move. This sound is believed to ward off evil spirits.

Choose one dancer to be the Leader, someone with a good sense of rhythm. She will lead the line of women. Everyone else needs to watch her and follow her cues. Her bearing (and the bearing of all the dancers) should be proud and tall, and the dance is done with quiet dignity. The men shake rattles and sing as the women dance.

1 Join the ribbons now, ee-ee oh-oh,
ah-ah, hay-yay—
With the ribbons dance, ee-ee oh, ah-ah,
hay-yay—

2 Join the ribbons now, ee-ee oh-oh,
ah-ah, hay-yay—
For the corn give thanks, ee-ee oh,
ah-ah, hay-yay—

3 Join the ribbons now, ee-ee oh-oh
ah-ah, hay-yay—
Praise we offer thee, ee-ee oh-oh, ah,
hay-yay!

4 With the ribbons dance, ee-ee oh, ah-ah,
hay-yay!

For the corn give thanks, ee-ee oh,
ah-ah, hay-yay!
Praise we offer thee, ee-ee oh,
ah-ah, hay-yay!

All the women start in single file, Indian-style formation. Step forward on a flat foot, bending your knees slightly with each step, and gradually form a circle. You don't need to accomplish this in any particular amount of time; the music just repeats until you're finished. How long it can go depends on the size of the group. Take it at a leisurely pace. The speed will build gradually as the dance progresses.

Continue to walk, going halfway around the circle. Then the Leader faces the circle center. Everyone follows her lead. They all move toward it, and then go back to place with the same step.

For the last line of music (stanza 4), step to the left with your left foot. Then close with your right foot (in a sideways step). Bend your knees slightly with each step. Keep moving around the circle as you do it, and continue as long as you want. As you repeat this stanza, the momentum builds, controlled by the Leader.

The Leader signals when the dance is over by standing very still. The other dancers, watching her carefully, immediately stop their movements. When everyone has stood still for a few seconds, the dance is over.

TURKEY IN THE STRAW

Number of players: 8-Unlimited

This American classic is one of the best-loved songs of the Western frontier. It has hundreds of verses, most of them funny, silly and playful. Here are a few samples. After you've sung your fill, square up your sets and do a square dance to this music which sounds like an Irish jig.

I

I went out to milk and I didn't know how,
So I milked the goat instead of the cow.
Saw a turkey sittin' on a pile of straw,
A-winkin' at his mother-in-law.

CHORUS

Turkey in the straw *(echo:* Turkey in the straw),
Turkey in the hay *(echo:* Turkey in the hay),
Roll 'em up and twist 'em up a high tuck-a-haw,
And hit 'em with a tune they call Turkey in the Straw!

II

I met an old catfish swimmin' in the stream.
I asked that old catfish "What do you mean?"
I grabbed that catfish right by the snout
And turned Mister Catfish wrongside out!

CHORUS

III

I love to go a-fishin' on a bright summer day
To see the perches and the catfish play,
With their hands in their pockets and their pockets in their pants.
Would you like to see the fishes do the hootchie-kootchie dance?

CHORUS

IV

Well, if frogs had wings and snakes had hair
And automobiles went a-flying through the air
Well, if watermelons grew on the huckleberry vine,
We'd have winter in the summer time.

CHORUS

V

Oh, there once was a man with a double chin,
Who performed with skill on the violin.
Well, he played in time and he played in tune,
But he only could fiddle by the light of the moon!

CHORUS

VI

Oh, I went to Toledo and I walked around the block,
And I walked right into the baker's shop.
And I took two doughnuts out of the grease,
And I handed the lady there a five-cent piece.

TURKEY IN THE STRAW (continued)

TURKEY IN THE STRAW (continued)

Oh, she looked at the nickel, and she looked at me,
And she said, "This money is no good to me.
There's a hole in the middle and it goes right through."
Says I, "There's a hole in the doughnut, too!"

CHORUS

This dance is done in a square, with four couples forming its sides. They all face the center of the square. The couple that has its back to the music is the head couple. The man stands on the left, the lady on the right.

The calls for this dance can be spoken as the music plays, so you have as much time as you need for each step.

Oh, the first couple out to the couple
on the right—

The head couple, holding hands, moves out to the next couple on their right, and joins hands with that couple.

And you circle eight hands with
all your might.

Now they circle in four steps—moving halfway around so that the head couple ends up facing the circle center. All still hold hands.

TURKEY IN THE STRAW (continued)

Now you duck for the oyster—

The second couple lifts their clasped hands to form an arch. The head couple walks under the arch (with three steps) and then walks backwards from it.

And you dive for the clam!

Now the head couple makes an arch and the second couple walks through it and back out again.

And pass right through to the promised land!

The second couple makes an arch again, but this time, when the head couple goes under it, they drop hands with the second couple and go right back to their starting place.

CHORUS

Now you swing your partner up and down
And you swing her all around the town.
Just swing her high and swing her low,
Now catch your breath and here we go!

Back in place, each couple swings for the first three lines of the chorus. On the fourth line, they stop and stand in place. Don't forget to sing the chorus each time you dance it.

Children under eight: Give your partner both hands and skip around each other in place.

Everyone over eight: Partners put right feet near each other, hold their arms in a really stretched-out dance position, and look at each other over their right shoulders. Then they pivot around with the left foot, keeping the right foot pretty much in place.

The dance starts again, but this time the second couple goes out to the third, doing the same patterns that the head couple did before. Finally they get back to their original places and the chorus repeats, as everybody swings. The dance starts again with the third couple going out to the fourth. Remember to change the words of the call, so it becomes:

Oh, the second couple out to the couple on the right,

and then

Oh, the third couple out to the couple on the right,

After each couple has had its turn to dance with all the other couples, and you are doing the last chorus, change the words to:

Now you swing your partner up and down
And you swing her all around the town,
Just swing her high and swing her low,
And give her a hug before you go!

Holding hands is crucial to the success of this pattern. The head couple, Jason and Melanie, are making sure to keep hands joined with Jennifer and Robert, as well as with each other as they "duck for the oyster."

hanukkah hanukkah hanukkah hanukkah

HANUKKAH O HANUKKAH

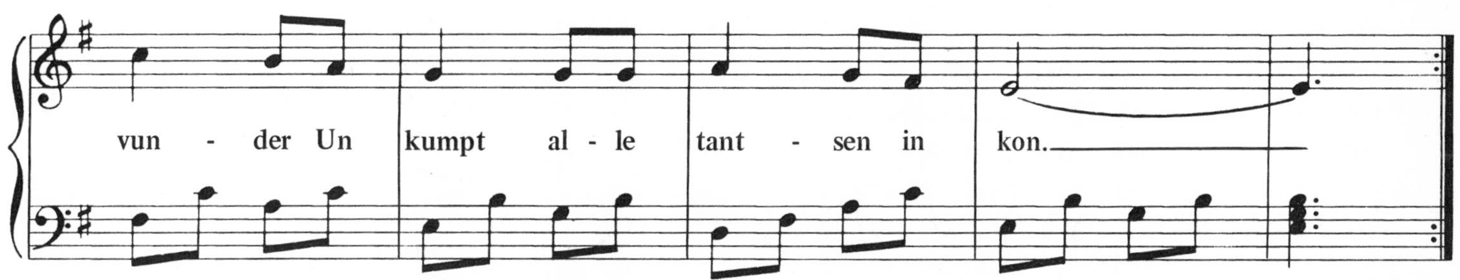

hanukkah hanukkah hanukkah hanukkah

HANUKKAH, O HANUKKAH

Number of players: 8-Unlimited

Hanukkah is the Jewish Festival of Lights, which is usually celebrated in December. It celebrates the miracle that took place in 165 B.C. when the Jews defeated the Syrian rulers and went to reclaim their Temple. Going to light the Temple lights, they found they had only one small earthen pot of oil, which would not last for more than a day. But the oil kept the lamp burning for eight days and nights, until new oil could be prepared. Thereafter, the festival of Hanukkah was observed every year.

It is a happy holiday, with special songs, special foods and presents for each of the eight nights that it lasts. This song tells about the delicious potato *latkes* (potato pancakes—pronounced LOT-kiss) that are served with applesauce or sour cream, and a special toy, which is a many-sided top called a *dreidel* (pronounced DRAY-dle). It's also about the eight Hanukkah candles in the *menorah* (a special candle holder). One candle is lit for each of the eight nights of the holiday.

**O Hanukkah, O Hanukkah, a yontef a
sheyner,
A lustiger, a freylicher, nito noch azeiner.
Ale nacht in dreydlach shpilen mir
Zudig heyse latkes est on a shir.
Geshvinder, tzindt kinder, di dininke
lichtelech on.
Zul yeder bazunder bazingen dem vunder
Un kumt alle tantsen in kon.
Zul yeder bazunder bazingen dem vunder
Un kumt alle tantsen in kon.**

If you want to sing it in English, you can sing:

**O Hanukkah, O Hanukkah, a festival of joy,
A holiday, a jolly day, for every girl and boy.
Spin the whirling dreidel all week long.
Eat the sizzling latkes, sing the happy songs!
Now light then, tonight then, the flickering
candles in a row,
Retell the wondrous story of God in all His
glory,
And dance by the candles' cheering glow.**

The dance incorporates many of the elements of Hanukkah: the feeling of joy, the spinning of the dreidels, and the lighting of the Hanukkah candles. Any number of partners may dance. If the group is not too large, do it in a long line, with partners facing each other. If the group is large,

These Hannukah dreidels are certainly serious about spinning. Evelyn (second from the left) has her feet too far apart—that slows her down. Feet should be together, close to your partner's feet. Then, as you pull away from from your partner, you form a strong base to spin from.

HANUKKAH O HANUKKAH (continued)

have the partners make a circle, so that one partner is facing the circle center, and the other has his or her back to it and is looking at the partner. You can vary the way you do the dance. It works either way.

O Hanukkah, O Hanukkah, a yontef a sheyner,

Hold your partner's hands and slide eight times in whatever direction the Leader chooses, either in a line or around the circle.

A lustiger, a freylicher, nito noch azeiner

Repeat the same slides, but this time, change direction, so that you end up where you started.

Ale nacht in dreydlach shpilen mir

Put your arms all the way around your partner's waist, and clasp your own hands together behind your partner's back with a strong grasp. Your partner does the same thing. Then, leaning away from each other, you spin around like a top—a dreidel. Keep your feet close together so that you have a solid base to spin from. You no longer need to stay in line. Spin anywhere in the room, passing the other dreidels as you whirl.

Zudig heyse latkes est on a shir.

In the same position, stop and spin in the other direction, so you don't get dizzy.

Geshvinder, taindt kinder, di dininke lichtelech on.

Drop hands. Make believe that you are holding the *shamos* (the candle that is used to light the Hanukkah candles), and that there is a menorah in front of you.

Pantomime lighting the first candle, and then continue with similar movements until all the candles are lit. Turn your head a little each time you light the next candle, so it's clear that you are focusing on it. This is a slow and solemn movement, and it should be done with dignity.

Zul yeder bazunder bazingen dem vunder
Un kumt alle tantsen in kon.
Zul yeder bazunder bazingen dem vunder
Um kumt alle tantsen in kon.

Now dance alone, as the spirit moves, making your way back to your starting position by the end of the song. Face your partner and get ready to start the dance from the beginning.

HURRY LITTLE HORSEY!

Number of players: 4-Unlimited

This simple Christmas chant comes from Montevideo on the southern coast of Uruguay. The town is called the "City of Roses," because of the many thousands of roses that cover its parks and gardens. Its people celebrate Christmas in the same way that we do: being with their families and exchanging presents.

Hurry, little horsey,
On to Bethlehem.
Tomorrow's a fiesta—
It's Christmas time again.

Hurry, little horsey,
Hurry, hurry on!
If we're late to the fiesta,
We will miss the jolly fun.

You can also use this rhyme to joggle a child on your knee. It has a great bouncing rhythm!

¡Arre, caballito!
Vamos al Belén,
Que mañana es fiesta
Y pasado también.

¡Arre, caballito!
Caballito arre!
Que si no a la fiesta
Llegaremos tarde.

Partners are horses and riders. The "horse" stands in front of the "rider" with arms stretched out in back. The rider takes the outstretched hands and they gallop around the room. Three- and four-year-olds can just gallop forward. Five-year-olds and older players can make the galloping into a pattern:

HURRY LITTLE HORSEY! (continued)

Hurry, little horsey,

Gallop four times forward.

On to Bethlehem,

Gallop four times backwards.

Tomorrow's a fiesta—
It's Christmas time again!

Gallop eight times forward.

Repeat this pattern for the second stanza. Since the first stanza ends with eight gallops forward, and the second starts with four gallops forward, the horses are actually doing twelve gallops at a time.

Note: Don't forget to reverse parts so that everyone has a chance to be both horse and rider.

If you're working with an older group (age seven and up) and feeling adventurous, skip the riders and try organizing a team of horses. Carry out the same pattern, but start with four horses, each holding onto the waist of the one in front. If that works (it's tricky to reverse direction with so many horses involved), try hitching two teams of horses together, so you have a team of eight. And if you're successful enough not to have them all fall down, try it with sixteen—and good luck!

CHRISTMAS LUAU

Number of players: 4-Unlimited

In ancient Hawaii there was no written language, so stories and poems and historical events were passed from generation to generation through chants called *olis* and dances called *hulas*, which is the Hawaiian word for dances and dancing.

This modern hula, based on "A Visit from St. Nicholas" by Clement Moore, or, as it's often called, "'Twas the night before Christmas," tells what a Hawaiian family does at Christmas. It describes many old Hawaiian traditions which live on.

You will be doing the basic hula step from side to side. Stand in a line, next to each other with space between.

THE BASIC HULA STEP

Foot Movements: These are easy. With your right foot, take a small step to the right. Now bring your left foot over to the right foot and step on it. Take another small step to the right with your right foot, and bring your left foot over again, but this time, don't step on it. Just touch it to the ground, so that your weight remains on your right foot. The basic hula step takes four counts:

Right-Together-Right-Touch
Left-Together-Left-Touch.

Bend your knees a little, which enables your hips to move. Keep the hip movement small; don't exaggerate it.

This foot pattern repeats throughout the hula, so practice it until it becomes natural and you can do it without thinking.

Arm Movements: These arm movements require much more attention, so make sure you have the foot movements down pat before continuing. Your arms should move in a soft, undulating way, like a gentle wave, rolling. The movements go from your fingers, into your wrists and elbows.

Remember that the movements of Hawaiian hulas are soft and gentle. Your hands and fingers should move easily and gracefully, as should your hips. Use lazy, slow movements, like the soft Hawaiian ocean breezes.

Note: The Hawaiian alphabet has only twelve letters and every Hawaiian word and syllable ends with a vowel. Two consonants are never without a vowel between them, and the accent is usually on the next to last syllable. Each sound is clearly pronounced, such as the familiar word *aloha* (ah-LOW-ha) which means "greetings" or "welcome."

Costume note: It adds a great deal of color if all the dancers wear leis, which are wreaths, usually made of flowers strung together, that reach to the waist. You can make them by cutting crepe paper circles of different colors about six to eight inches in diameter. Pinch them in the center so they resemble flowers, and string them with a needle on a strong piece of string or yarn. Leis should be about three feet long. If you want, put the flowers only on the part that shows in the front. If you want to be authentic, put flowers all around.

Girls wear muumuus, which are long, loose flowing dresses of many bright colors. A short colorful nightgown might do the trick. Boys can wear colorful Hawaiian shirts, leis, and a scarf tied around their hips to resemble a *malo*, which is a loincloth.

The chart which follows shows you what to do with words, feet, arms and hands on each individual line.

christmas christmas christmas christmas

CHRISTMAS LUAU

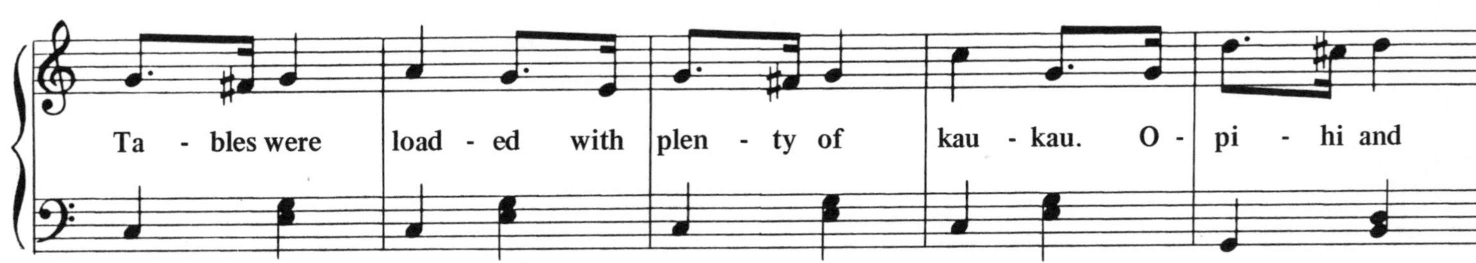

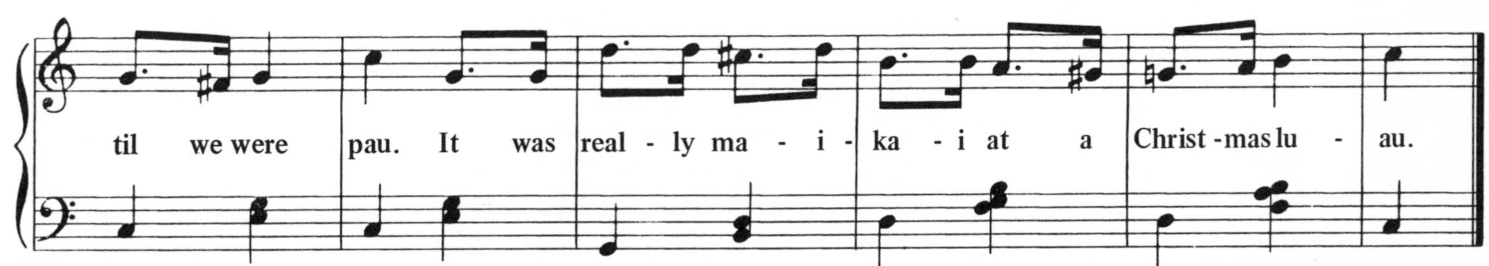

christmas christmas christmas christmas

CHRISTMAS LUAU (continued)

WORDS	FEET	ARMS	HANDS
'Twas the night before Christmas,	hula right	arms high overhead	Wave hands together, then apart, and wave again.
and all through the *hale* (house),	hula left	hands in front of chest, elbows up	Put finger tips together to form a thatched roof.
there was singing and dancing	hula right	left hand on hip	Right hand waves to mouth to signify singing, and then lowers to front of chest.
and *hoomalimali* (flattery).	hula left	Cross your arms in front of your chest, with elbows down and fingers up.	Fingers wave twice.
Mama in her *muumuu*	hula right	Girls with a gracious wave of the entire arm, point to their dress from the top to the bottom. Boys point to the girls with pride.	Fingers wave with the arm.
and me in my *malo* (loincloth)	hula left	Boys point to malo; girls point to boys with pride.	Fingers wave with the pointing arm.
were greeting *aikanes* (friends)	hula right	Both hands wave to the mouth and then are stretched out in front, as though throwing a kiss.	Fingers wave.

CHRISTMAS LUAU (continued)

WORDS	FEET	ARMS	HANDS
with "*pehea, mahalo*" ("How are you, Thank you").	hula left	Lift up the lei and hold it out, in a gesture of giving.	
Sister gathered flowers	hula right	Left hand is cupped in front of the waist, palm up. Right hand picks flowers out to the right and puts them in the basket.	Right hand waves as it picks flowers.
for a lei.	hula left	Wave hands twice to the lei that you are wearing.	Fingers wave.
Brother watched the *imu* (underground oven)	hula right	Put fingers of right hand under chin. Left hand is under right elbow, which is parallel to floor.	
all through the day.	hula left	Hold the same position as above.	
Soon the music boys	hula right	Hold out left arm as if holding a ukelele.	Fingers of right hand strum the ukelele.
began to play	hula left	Continue with same movement.	Continue strumming the uke.
***meles* (songs or chants) old and new**	hula right	Both hands wave to the mouth and again out front.	Fingers wave.

CHRISTMAS LUAU (continued)

WORDS	FEET	ARMS	HANDS
of Hawaii *nei* (all of Hawaii).	hula left	Hold left hand high over head, and right hand in front of waist. Turn palms up and bring arms out to side.	
Tables were loaded	hula right	Hands are palm down in front of waist. Separate them bringing them straight out to the sides.	
with plenty of *kaukau* (food).	hula left	Left hand in front of waist, palm touching belly.	Rub right hand in circular motion over left as if to say "yum yum."
***Opihi* (shellfish) and salmon**	hula right	Left hand is cupped, palm up in front of waist. Right hand is up.	Middle finger and thumb form a shellfish. Then bring right hand to left with fingers straight across and palm in, signifying the salmon swimming.
in steaming hot *laulau* (the plant leaves that the food is wrapped in).	hula left	Left hand stays cupped in front of waist.	Right hand peels leaves from food in left hand.

CHRISTMAS LUAU (continued)

WORDS	FEET	ARMS	HANDS
We ate and told stories	hula right	Still holding the left hand cupped in front of waist, eat poi (a starchy food made by pounding the root of the taro plant, making it into a paste).	Scoop the forefinger and middle finger of right hand to left hand and mouth.
until we were *pau* (finished or done).	hula left	Puff out tummy and bring both hands in big circle in front of waist.	
It was really *maika'i* (good or wonderful)	hula right	With both hands slap hips, clap hands in front of chest and snap fingers at sides of head. This needs to be done quickly.	
at a Christmas *luau* (feast).	END THE DANCE WITH THE HAWAIIAN PAU		

THE HAWAIIAN PAU

The Hawaiian Pau is a bow. It goes like this:

1. Step on your left foot and bend your knee.
2. Extend your right foot, but don't put your weight on it.
3. Cross your arms in front of your chest, elbows bent, with the fingers and thumb of the right hand resting on the fingers and thumb of the left hand. Curl your fingers upward.
4. Holding your back straight, bow your head.

ESTA NOCHE ES NOCHE BUENA (New Year's Eve)

ESTA NOCHE ES NOCHE BUENA (New Year's Eve)

Number of players: 6-Unlimited

This traditional New Year's Eve song comes from central Spain, and you need pennies for it. Try to collect new shiny ones; their sparkle adds to the feeling of celebration.

Choose one person to be the Mayor, who is important and stands on one side of the room, with a basket or bowl full of the pennies. The Mayor can preen and puff up, acting rich and powerful. If you have an important-looking hat and cloak, let the Mayor wear them and he or she will feel more like playing the part.

The others walk around the room singing the song:

Esta noche es Noche Buena,
Y mañana es Año Nuevo.
Iremos a dar los dias,
Al señor alcalde nuevo.
Danos, danos, danos, si nos has de dar,
Que es la noche corta y hay mucho que andar.

which means

Tonight is New Year's Eve
And tomorrow is New Year's Day.
We are on our way to greet the Mayor, and we say,
"Give us, give us lots of pennies,
Hear our song, for the night is short and the way is long."

When the singers come to the part that says, "Danos, danos, danos," they stop before the Mayor who gives out the pennies. The Mayor can give each person one penny, or two or three or a handful, depending on how many are in the procession and how many pennies there are. The more pennies, the more important and rich is the Mayor.

Note: If the Mayor hasn't finished giving out the pennies by the end of the song (this will depend on the size of the group and how quickly the Mayor works) just repeat the last two lines, from the "danos" part. Let the Mayor dole out the pennies with ease and graciousness, as befits that station, without rushing.

The Mayor then collects the pennies back into the bowl or basket, gives it to the person who has been chosen to be the new Mayor, and the game repeats.

If you're playing the game with very young children (two-, three- or four-years-old), it might be a good idea for an adult to play the part of the Mayor. By five-years-old, children can handle the part of the Mayor, and love doing it.

AGE RANGES

	AGES 2	3	4	5	6	7	8
Captain Jinks of the Horse Marines				*	*	*	*
Christmas Luau					*	*	*
Creek Ribbon Dance					*	*	*
Dayenu				*	*	*	*
Easter Eggs Are Rolling	*	*	*	*	*	*	*
Esta Noche Es Noche Buena	*	*	*	*	*	*	*
Ghost Song					*	*	*
Gypsy in da Moonlight			*	*	*	*	*
Hanukkah O Hanukkah				*	*	*	*
Hurry Little Horsey!	*	*	*	*	*	*	*
I Don't Want No More of Army Life					*	*	*
I'm a Nut		*	*	*	*	*	*
Irish Trot					*	*	*
Ja Posejah Lubenice				*	*	*	*
Masked Valentines			*	*	*	*	*
New Year's Bells			*	*	*	*	*
Old Woman's Courtship			*	*	*	*	*
Out with Winter				*	*	*	*
Planting Rice			*	*	*	*	*
St. Patrick's Potato Race		*	*	*	*	*	*
There Was a Man and He Was Mad		*	*	*	*	*	*
There Was an Old Witch			*	*	*	*	*
Turkey in the Straw†				*	*	*	*
Twelve Little Rabbits		*	*	*	*	*	*
Wind Up the May Tree					*	*	*

†in multiples of 8, to form squares.

INDEX